Conspiracy Theorists and Logic: An Essay

Dawn D. Boyer, Ph.D.

Book Copyright: 2017© by Dawn D. Boyer, Ph.D.

ISBN Numbers: ISBN-13: 978-1-948149-07-5
ISBN-10: 1-948149-07-9

Copyright Notice: The Author supports copyright. Copyright sparks creativity, encourages diverse viewpoints, promotes free speech, and creates a vibrant and rich art culture. Thank you for buying an authorized copy of this copyrighted book and for complying with international copyright laws. All copyrights are reserved. No part of this book, including interior design, cover design, icons, and pictures may be reproduced or transmitted in any form by any means (electronic, photocopying, recording, or otherwise) without the prior written permission of the copyright owner. Independent of the author's economic rights, and even after the transfer of the said rights, the author shall have the right to claim authorship of the work and to object to any distortion, modification of, and/or other derogatory action in relation to the said work that could be deemed prejudicial to the author's honor or reputation No part of this book or images – black and white, or other renditions of images, are to be posted to any social media, Internet, and/or other digital media or platforms without prior written permission of the copyright owner You are supporting writers and allowing the author to continue to publish books for every other reader to continue to enjoy.

Trademarks: All brand names, product names, logos, service marks, trademarks, or registered trademarks are trademarks of their respective owners.

Author's Business Website www.DBoyerConsulting.com
Amazon Author Page: https://www.amazon.com/author/dawnboyer
Review Author's Books: www.shelfari.com/DawnDeniseBoyer
Facebook Author's Page: www.facebook.com/DawnBoyerAuthor
Facebook Business Page: www.Facebook.com/DBoyerConsulting
Google+ Business Page: https://plus.google.com/112802498128568560150/about?hl=en
LinkedIn www.linkedin.com/in/DawnBoyer

Conspiracy Theorists and Logic

I can't believe I am still hearing about these ridiculous conspiracy theories continuing to be shared on Social Media, as well as semi-Main Stream Media (MSM), popping up in my news feeds with sensationalized headlines and acting for all intents and purposes like view-suckers for a huge listing of online advertising. I keep shaking my head at the National Enquirerer-like headlines with so little content to explain the headline; I kept wondering why on earth am I wasting my time clicking through (and have stopped).

So I thought, without any 'conspiracy proofs' but mostly conjecture, could I explain away the conspiracies rampant in the Internet Universe? You have seen the headlines ...

- Pharmas are only out to make money off sick people and create drugs to keep them sick ...
- The United States Government planned and carried out the 9/11 attacks because the buildings would not have collapsed as a result of the airplane fuel explosion ...
- President Kennedy's assassination was planned by Lyndon B. Johnson and the CIA and/or there was a second shooter on the grassy knoll ...
- Water condensation trails ('contrails') from aircraft secretly consist of chemical or biological agents used to ...

- The Sandy Hook school massacre was a false story that misled the media, and not a single person died that day because it was a practice event for local police …
- Barack Obama was born in Kenya and thus was an illicit president …
- Pizzagate was a pizza restaurant connected to members of the Democratic Party with a (non-existent) child-sex ring

Regardless of the conspiracy theorists' charges' and 'proofs' (which are links to crazy left-winger websites where someone is making accusations but never any real, scientific proof, or valid names (always a first name and last name initial or 'anonymous'), one needs to think out the logic of the claim. I am so done with the click-bait sites that post sensationalist headlines, and when you click through, they don't even showcase what the headline is about, and you have to click through endless pages of advertisements for weight loss and movie star gossip.

So, let's logically walk through the listed conspiracies to ask some questions that may answer whether the conspiracy theorist's claims are valid in the first place ...

- Pharmas are only out to make money off sick people and create drugs to keep them sick...

What conspiracy theorists are insinuating is pharmaceutical companies are so focused on profits and revenue that they create drugs that make folks sick or sicker. They will never strive to find a cure for cancer or AIDS because they have no incentive –

once the folks are cured, there is no more incentive to purchase the drugs; thus, the Pharmas will then lose profits and go under.

Conspiracy theorists are not taking into account the thousands of scientists and doctors who are working for the Pharma who have family members with diseases and illnesses such as cancer, tumors, and other genetic health issues that take value away from their loved ones' lives. If I was a research doctor for a Pharma, and my child got cancer, I would want to work my arse off to help the R&D team find a cure so my child could get well, and the discoveries that cured my child could help other children (and adults). If I were a research doctor for a Pharma who was working on a vaccine for AIDS, when I had two family members who were gay and susceptible to the disease, I sure would work hard to create that cure or vaccine for the horrible disease. If I were a research doctor for Pharma who was working on a cure or treatment for Alzheimer's, I would give a body part to be on the team to find the cure, knowing that with my family's history of the disease, I could personally be at risk for this nasty, crippling, evil disease.

    Once the 'cure' or 'treatment' is found, of course, the Pharmas are going to charge an arm and a leg for it because they invested millions, if not hundreds of millions, into finding that cure – salary, expensive lab equipment and facilities, and Pharmas aren't in business to do things for free. Pharma companies must pay workers, including the CEOs, who spend a lifetime managing a profitable business for stockholders and are appropriately compensated for their knowledge. Pharmas must pay for marketing and advertising to promote the drug. Pharmacists have to go through trials and applications via government agencies to get approval to sell the drug to the public, sometimes taking years for approvals after data submitted from research trials on animals to get to the human subject testing stage. Pharmas have to develop specialized, security-based, shipping and handling methods because a truckload of a drug could be valued in the 'millions' for delivery to pharmacy warehouses and prone to hijacking. By the time many drugs get to market, the Pharma may be in the 'red' for expenses to support this drug and have only ten years to make up for the losses and start making a profit before they are forced to allow generic brands on the market from their competitors.

So yes, Pharmas are in business to make money, but no, pharmas don't purposefully *not* create a cure or treatment for a disease to continue to make money. Their incentive is to make a profit to keep employees working, scientists researching, providing drugs to health care practitioners for their patients, and hopefully to find a cure in the process – not only for the public market but ALSO for their loved ones who are part of that public market.

Conspiracy theorists are also not taking into account that most folks on the planet are honest workers, ethical and professional, and have good intentions for their fellow man. Most human beings have a hard time keeping a secret … so if there is an overt and true conspiracy to keep drug cures from reaching the public market, don't you think that many of those decent human beings will make a fuss and report the cure to the public and government officials who will do a little digging and then find out the Pharma may not have been reporting all their human subject ethical treatment or that they have discovered a cure. Something GOOD will NOT remain a secret forever!

So think about it: what is the real incentive for a Pharma to find a cure or not find a cure and then not shout it from the rooftops to gain more market branding for their drug lineup and the 'cure' when there will be a massive rush to the gate to get the drugs by folks and their families to obtain that magic drug?

- The United States Government planned and carried out the 9/11 attacks because the buildings would not have collapsed as a result of the airplane fuel explosion ...

This simply can't be true ... the number of government officials who were in the World Trade Center (WTC) at the time of the crashes, and the almost 2,000 plus lives lost that day, would have meant that someone would have known a friend or family member who would have been in danger of being caught in the mess or dying as a result of the accident. A new high-level official of the Homeland Security Department had been in his brand new office in the WTC for 1-2 days and knew there was something big being planned by Osama Bin Laden very soon. Still, he wasn't sure what the event would be or where. Do you not think if he or the US government had known anything, he would have known it and would have stayed home from work that day?

Steel is just the element iron that has been processed to control the amount of carbon. Out of the ground, iron melts at around 1,510 degrees C (2750°F). Steel often melts at approximately 1,370 degrees C (2500°F).[i] The individual metal components of the airplanes that struck the WTC buildings are comparable in strength to the box perimeter columns of the WTC, which is the keel beam at the bottom of the aircraft fuselage. The aircraft impact essentially destroyed multiple columns in the WTC perimeter wall, and the loads were shifted to the remaining columns in the highly redundant structure. The explosion was of equal or even greater significance during this initial impact when 90,000 L gallons of jet fuel, comprising nearly 1/3 of the aircraft's weight, ignited. The ensuing fire was the principal cause of the collapse.[ii] The WTC fire was fuel-rich – hardly surprising, with 90,000 L of jet fuel. Flame volume and quantity of soot increased the radiative heat loss in the fire, moving the temperature closer to the maximum of 1,000°C. Still, it was unlikely the WTC steel experienced temperatures above the 750–800°C range.

    Christian Simensen, from a Norwegian research institute, SINTEF, theorizes that molten aluminum from aircraft bodies mixed with water from the sprinkler systems catalyzed secondary blasts that brought the WTC down. Simensen's idea: after the planes impacted the WTC towers, tons of molten aluminum ran down the floors below the impact sites, mingling with hundreds of liters of water from the buildings' fire sprinkler systems. This mix of aluminum and water is known to cause a chemical reaction that can boost temperatures and put off combustible hydrogen in the process. It's a recipe for a hot explosion.[iii]

So the bottom line is it was most likely not the building's steel that melted and caused the collapses ... it was likely the aluminum that the airplanes were built with, combined with water and the diesel fuel spilled from the airplanes, combined in the lethal mix that did eventually bring down the two skyscrapers.

A constant domino chain of events started with the Pilot Training Center. The terrorists received training on take-offs and flying those jetliners but never showed any interest in signing up for the class(es) on landing those aircraft. Yes, there are much stricter regulations about folks who want to take those types of piloting classes in place now, and many more questions are asked on the applications, as well as potential mandated requirements for background checks.

Only one person can keep a secret unless the second or third person who knows the secret is dead. Again, most folks on the planet are honest workers, ethical and professional, and have good intentions for their fellow man. Most human beings have a pretty hard time keeping a secret ... so after a decade and a half since the event of 9/11 ... not one valid piece of proof has come out of the woodwork that can scientifically and reliably prove that the US government (as a whole or individuals) was directly or holistically responsible for the attacks on the World Trade Center buildings.

- President Kennedy's assassination was

planned by Lyndon B. Johnson and the CIA, and/or there was a second shooter on the grassy knoll …

As a young child in elementary school, I remember coming home on that December day to excitedly announce to my mother that "someone shot President Lincoln!" getting everything mixed up on what had happened. Confusion prevailed, and police investigative procedures and tactics were in their infancy. Of course, the news media were also confused about what happened, when, and how and reported what they could gather. It wasn't hard to make educated (or uneducated) guesses based on rumors and gossip that eventually grew in epic proportions to mythical truths. The most recent release of government investigative records, photos, and other documents that have been under lock and key from the investigation for over four decades were released in 2017 (Presidential Order by Donald Trump) to the eager hands of conspiracy theorists, historians, and other researchers to look deeper into those documents for the answers to the questions they had been asking for decades.

  Conspiracists link John F. Kennedy's death to the cover-up of his affair with Marilyn Monroe, LBJ's attempt to wrest the presidency from the young Catholic upstart, or the CIA being upset with secrets that JFK was going to release to the public and other theories. Lee Harvey Oswald was an angry, self-proclaimed communist sympathizer who had it out for JFK and had the perfect opportunity to assassinate the young president. He coincidentally also had a sniper's training and experience to carry out the job. All the dominoes fell in place for the success of this horrible event.

It is a shame Oswell was killed before being interviewed so the police could obtain more answers to their questions, but if the CIA were involved, would not one person come out on their deathbed to relate any 'secrets' about the government's involvement in the assassination at this late date? There simply can not be anyone with any ethical or Christian upbringing who would not step up and protest some or all of any attempts to kill the president or not slip and talk about such conspiracy with any valid connections to the operators of this conspiracy in all these years.

- Water condensation trails ('contrails') from aircraft secretly consist of chemical or biological agents used to …

Those airplanes supposedly 'secretly' spraying chemicals (if their intent) can easily create refrigeration for those chemicals to secretly spray those chemicals without the contrails showing. Wouldn't that make more sense? Conspiracy theorists always propose the most outlandish events, but don't give those supposedly doing these events any credit for brilliance to avoid being detected. They secretly plan these events and are brilliant enough to hide their activities, but aren't smart enough to hide their illegal activities. It's a catch-22 of logical nonsense.

Yes, there are events where an airplane's toilet tank spigots or traps become broken and spill waste into the air. Still, those events usually occur so high up over the earth's surface any spillage is dissipated quickly and in such a broad area, the minute particles resulting from the spill would be milligrams in size by the time it reached the earth's surface, as well as potentially evaporating before it even reached that point.

    So, what chemicals would be productive to spray on the general population? Poisons? Mind-control drugs? Nuclear-waste? If poison, was it the type that could easily be wiped off if it landed on anyone's skin? If it is mind-control drugs, wouldn't a person have to have a higher dose intravenously for it to work? If nuclear waste, what type of nuclear waste? Three types of solid nuclear wastes are classified in terms of their radioactivity, e.g., low, intermediate, and high-level wastes, and low-level wastes just need paper suits to avoid contamination. The government has intense standards and requirements for nuclear waste storage and dispersal. How would it get past those compliance standards to be loaded into an airplane at a massive enough quantity to do any damage to the general population?

What airline pilot would sign up for a 'dump' of hazardous chemicals, knowing if the plane had to crash-land (where pilot and passengers survived), the chemicals would spill all over the landscape where they landed (or even splash on them while flying the plane)? I am pretty sure any pilot for any flight knows precisely what is onboard their plane at any given time. I am pretty sure any commercial airline, after all the current USA security measures, would know exactly what, if any, hazardous materials may be onboard. No commercial plane I know of has the capability to dump hazardous materials or chemicals. The only capability they would have to dump anything would be jet fuel directly from the plane's fuel tanks. No one would substitute HAZMAT chemicals in a fuel tank for an airplane because the airplane wouldn't be able to take off with no real fuel in the tank, right? One would have to use a specially designed airplane to spray chemicals from a ballast tank to spread the chemicals in the air, right?

What makes more sense? Condensation trails from the difference in temperatures of the air at the level the plane is traveling - or - are chemicals purposefully being spilled onto the planet on purpose?

- The Sandy Hook school massacre was a false story that misled the media, and not a single person died that day because it was a practice event for local police …

Twenty students and six adults were killed at Sandy Hook Elementary School on December 14, 2012, by a 20-year-old shooter. The false rumors that the FBI reported no deaths in that geographic area (Newtown, CT, USA) supposedly proved the news story of these shootings as being false.

It is well known that the FBI collects shooting statistics but is often months, if not years, behind in reporting back to public forums. This also may stem from local law enforcement not reporting statistics and data promptly or lacking administrative personnel. It takes months or years to report the data to the FBI for data compilation in a national database.

Why would the media have helicopters hovering overhead, thousands of feet of video film, and thousands of photos of the parents behind the police lines waiting to hear about their child and wondering if their son or daughter were alive or dead? What purpose would there be to having the media 'in on the conspiracy'? What would be the media motive? The media would be the first folks to report there was a conspiracy!

The motive, according to conspiracy theorists, was the media was colluding with authorities, local citizens, local police, and politicians to persuade Americans with another reason to give up their guns.[iv]

This conspiracy theory offends not only the parents who have lost their children in this horrid event but offends the intelligence of the American people, who can see with their own eyes as the aftermath was shown on television for weeks. There is not one person who has come forward with valid credentials or documentation. This shooting event was a practice for local law enforcement or an elaborate hoax.

- Barack Obama was born in Kenya and thus was an illicitly elected president ...

I shake my head at all those who claim that Barack Obama was not eligible to be President of the USA because he was supposedly born in Kenya. For conspiracy theorists who are still on the bandwagon, you need to go back to review your American Constitutional Law and policy on eligibility to run for president of the United States.

Article Two of the United States Constitution establishes the executive branch of the federal government, which carries out and enforces federal laws. The executive branch includes the President, the Vice

President, the Cabinet, executive departments, independent agencies, and other boards, commissions, and committees. Section 1 of Article Two of the United States Constitution sets forth the eligibility requirements for serving as president of the United States: No Person except a natural-born Citizen or a Citizen of the United States, at the time of the Adoption of this Constitution, shall be eligible to the Office of President; neither shall any person be eligible to that Office who shall not have attained to the Age of thirty-five Years, and been fourteen Years a Resident within the United States. At the time the President takes office, he must be (a) a natural-born citizen, (b) at least 35 years old, and (c) an inhabitant of the United States for at least fourteen years. A person can become a U.S. citizen in one of four ways: (1) by being born in the United

States or one of its territories, (2) if born to parents who are U.S. citizens (acquisition of citizenship), (3) a citizen through the naturalization process (applying for, and passing, a citizenship test), and (4) a citizen if one or both of your parents have been naturalized (derivation of citizenship).[v]

For a person to be considered a Citizen of the United States of America, that person must have been born abroad in wedlock to two U.S. citizen parents.[vi] A person born abroad in wedlock to a U.S. citizen mother and a U.S. citizen father acquires U.S. citizenship at birth under section 301(c) of the Immigration and Nationality Act (INA) if one of the parents has had a residence in the United States or one of its outlying possessions before the person's birth.[vii]

Some conspiracy theorists claim that Obama, having supposedly been born outside the USA (Kenya), would have invalidated his citizenship at birth. The truth is, Obama would still be eligible for the presidency, regardless of where he was born. In the conspiracy theorist's hypothetical scenario, Obama was born outside the US, he could not be a natural-born citizen since the then-applicable law would have required Obama's mother to have been in the U.S. at least "five years after the age of 14," but his mother was three months shy of her 19th birthday when Obama was born.

So essentially, USA military-dependent parents stationed overseas in the UK, South Korea, Japan, and Germany, who give birth to children overseas (whether in foreign hospitals or on USA territory military bases), provide instant USA citizenship to those babies the minute they are born if one or both of the parents are USA citizens, simply as the babies' birthright. President Barack Obama's mother was a US citizen, even though his father was a dual citizen of the UK and Kenya. Regardless of where the president was born, he was – in turn – an automatic US citizen by birthright. Regardless, the birth certificate is (deemed valid by researchers) produced by the Hawaain hospital where he was born, and the newspapers running the birth story in the vital statistics pages in the week(s) after he was born support the president was born in the USA.

Story over, conspiracy disproved.

- Pizzagate was a pizza restaurant connected to members of the Democratic

Party with a human trafficking and a child-sex ring ...

In the fall of 2016, John Podesta's e-mail (Hillary Clinton's campaign manager) was hacked in a spear-phishing attack. Consequently, his private and business e-mails were made public by WikiLeaks. Proponents of the Pizzagate theory inferred the e-mails contained coded messages insinuating human trafficking and connecting restaurants in the USA and members of the Democratic Party with an alleged child-sex ring. The pizza restaurant that conspiracy theorists identified was Comet Ping Pong. Law enforcement organizations, including the DC Police Department, have discredited this child-sex-trafficking theory.

The restaurant's owner, James Alefantis, told the news media: "... we've come under constant assault. I've done nothing ... but try to clean this up and protect my staff and friends from being terrorized." On December 4, 2016, Edgar M. Welch, a 28-year-old Salisbury, NC man, fired three shots in the restaurant with an AR-15-style rifle, later telling police he had planned to 'self-investigate' the conspiracy theory. He surrendered to law enforcement after he "found no evidence that underage children were being harbored in the restaurant" and was arrested ... thankfully no one was injured.

Conclusion

So, while folks on social media continue to proclaim these false conspiracy theories are "true" based on what they have read and are promulgated via multiple websites (with non-valid resources) and social media 'shares,' it is wise to do several things if you want to share the information or continue to push the theory.

1) Check the resources of the information. Just because it was shared by your wife's second cousin's in-law doesn't make it true. Stop listening to gossip!

2) What is the reliability of the website where

you are researching and finding the information? If it's a commercial site talking about conspiracy theories in the first place, keep looking. If it's a site full of advertising for male enhancement boosters and weight loss products, keep looking.

3) The more important and valid resources for true story information are the mainstream news media non-editorials – meaning the nitty gritty who, what, where, when, why, and how stories of the event. Ignore pundits who provide opinions about the event. Ignore sensationalists who use slants to gain readership but ignore the real details of the story.

4) Look for police reports about the event. Some or all of the attending officers' reports

are or may be public documents before the courts get involved and contain the officer's viewpoint about what they saw throughout the event.

5) Look for autopsy reports – these are usually public documents on the cause of death, and in today's era, mandated via compliance to report any and all elements of the person's death. These can be ordered about 30-60 days after the death via a request form found on the state's Office of the Chief Medical Examiner and/or coroner's office website.

6) After you finish researching the 'open web,' try researching in the 'deep web' which is usually via academic and research libraries that make available journal articles and

research papers published by academic scholars who perform literature reviews, compile statistical facts, and then use quantitative (crunching numbers, testing for theories) or qualitative (interviewing real people) research which proves or disproves theories that may or may not support the conspiracy one is trying to research.

7) Look for official government reports from federal and state agencies who may be involved in recording or documenting the events.

8) Look for reports (or research) created by non-profit agencies that do not have biased or political leanings. Some agencies provide mandatory reports to their board of directors, and they must be publicly

available to anyone requesting the information.

Think Harder and Wiser For Yourself

Most importantly, ask yourself: Does this theory make sense? Would normal human beings with ethical and/or Christian backgrounds and upbringings do this sort of thing or try to hide something this awful or heinous? Would one who could know about this conspiracy keep a secret from the rest of the world? Would the only person who would know this 'secret' have a specific incentive to keep it a secret? If more than one person is involved in this event, how on earth could they 'all' keep the secret?

Remember, when you spread the conspiracy theory to others, you endanger your reputation as a realist or honest person. If someone I was close to started a campaign to prove the US Government took down the World Trade Towers, I would think they had a screw loose. Certainly, after the hundreds, if not thousands, of forensic scientists, have poured over all the evidence and provided their scientific and laboratory-based (in the field and in controlled lab conditions) conclusions, the conspiracies have been validly disproven.

ABOUT THE AUTHOR

Dawn D. Boyer, Ph.D. completed her Doctor of Philosophy in Education (Occupational & Technical Studies, with a concentration in Training & Development in Human Resources) from Old Dominion University in Norfolk, VA, in 2013. Her dissertation entitled, 'Competencies of Human Resources Practitioners within the Government Contracting Industry,' identified unique KSAs for Human Resources Managers working for federal-level government contracting companies. This groundbreaking research is the impetus of her recently released textbook guide for Human Resources Professionals in Government Contracting, available on Amazon.

She has been an entrepreneur and business owner for 14+ years, currently in her consulting firm, D. Boyer Consulting, based in

Richmond (Henrico County), VA, and servicing clients internationally. Her background experience is 24+ ars in the Human Resources field, of which 11 years are within the federal defense contracting industry.

Dr. Boyer's experience in federal (defense) contracting as a Human Resources Director or Senior Manager provided her a subject matter expert insight, experience, practice, and capabilities to perform within this industry, as well as the ability to instruct others to KSAs needed in middle-management or executive human resource roles.

Dr. Boyer works with job and new career seekers to write Search Engine Optimized resumes for increased visibility to recruiters – getting the candidates past the recruiting 'firewall' and interviewing for faster hires and job placement. Her tech-based knowledge of how the ATS software systems work helps job seekers in structuring a resume for recruiters' Boolean search queries. Her SEO coding within a resume is so unique, no other resume writers offer this service.

She assists academics and writers in publishing their works or manuscripts as a third-party publisher – DBC Publishing.

She is the author of over 1007 books on the topics of genealogy, family lineage, academic education, STEMPS education curriculum design, academic (Education) projects, human resources and government contracting, women and gender studies, business, and career search practice, quotes for self-improvement and motivation (2,000+ /3,000+ series), and her 'Interview with an Artist' series (three artists in the series to date). All her books are listed on her A zon author's page at: www.amazon.com/author/dawnboyer.

Dr. Boyer has been a member of LinkedIn since 2004 (a few months after the beta version was released) and has developed a rich profile for consistent and constant communications to ~12,800+ connections (as of Nov 2017). Her clients call her 'The Queen of LinkedIn.'

Interested in publishing your own academic essays, projects, or books? Contact the author for publishing project estimates, consulting, and assistance:

Dawn.Boyer@me.com
www.DBoyerConsulting.com

ABOUT THE BOOK

Dr. Boyer encounters a lot of conspiracy theories on social media and in ordinary conversations with peers and simply can't believe so many people are gullible to believe these crazy ideas instantly.

Being the logical person she is, she often asks realistic questions about the events and those who are conspiracy theory enthusiasts. She has more faith in her fellow human beings and Americans to believe many (or any) of the conspiracy theories floating around.

This short essay essentially asks those who hear the theories to stop, think, and logically work through not only the main-stream-media chatter but also if they want the answers to dig deeper into the truth that is documented by those who were there, scientists who do the research, and the authorities who search through the facts and sometimes the rubble to find the absolute truth about what happened.

No one can keep a secret if more than one person knows about events. Look at the laws and law enforcement documentation, research the scientific data, and understand other folks are human (and make mistakes, as well as have ethics in their lifestyles) before crying wolf in public.

Footnotes

---

i

https://www.google.com/search?q=steel+melts+at+what+temperature%3F&oq=steel+melts+at+what+temperature%3F&aqs=chrome..69i57.8534j0j7&sourceid=chrome&ie=UTF-8

ii

http://www.tms.org/pubs/journals/jom/0112/eagar/eagar-0112.html

iii

https://www.popsci.com/science/article/2011-09/new-theory-world-trade-center-collapse-blames-explosive-chemical-reaction

iv

https://www.snopes.com/info/news/sandyhoax.asp

v

http://immigration.findlaw.com/citizenship/u-s-citizenship-through-parents-or-by-birth.html

vi

https://www.google.com/search?source=hp&ei=QVYLWpjULJ2vjwTg5p6YBQ&q=citizenship+birth+requirements&oq=citizenship+eligibility+birth+&gs_l=psy-ab.3.0.0i22i30k1l2.888.12846.0.15511.47.39.5.0.0.0.276.4361.0j29j3.33.0....0...1.1.64.psy-ab..9.38.4524.6..0j46j35i39k1j0i131k1j0i46k1j0i67k1j0i20i263i264k1j0i20i264k1j0i46i67k1j46i67k1j0i10k1j0i20i263k1j33i22i29i30k1.113.oo2LfkoLUOE

vii

https://travel.state.gov/content/travel/en/legal-considerations/us-citizenship-laws-policies/citizenship-child-born-abroad.html

www.ingramcontent.com/pod-product-compliance
Lightning Source LLC
Chambersburg PA
CBHW060951050426
42453CB00009B/1153